FATHERED
BY
GOD

PARTICIPANT'S GUIDE

JOHN ELDREDGE

THOMAS NELSON
Since 1798

NASHVILLE   DALLAS   MEXICO CITY   RIO DE JANEIRO

Published in Nashville, Tennessee, by Thomas Nelson. Thomas Nelson is a trademark of Thomas Nelson, Inc.

The publisher is grateful to Craig McConnell for his writing skills and collaboration in developing the content for this book.

Published in association with Yates & Yates, LLP, Attorneys and Counselors, Orange, California.

Unless otherwise noted, Scripture quotations are from the HOLY BIBLE: NEW INTERNATIONAL VERSION®. © 1973, 1978, 1984 by International Bible Society. Used by permission of Zondervan Publishing House. All rights reserved.

Thomas Nelson, Inc., titles may be purchased in bulk for educational, business, fund-raising, or sales promotional use. For information, please e-mail SpecialMarkets@ThomasNelson.com.

ISBN: 978-1-4185-4289-4

Printed in the United States of America
10 11 12 13 RRD 5

CONTENTS

INTRODUCTION

You have made known to me the path of life;
you will fill me with joy in your presence,
with eternal pleasures at your right hand.
—Psalm 16:11

Show me your ways, O LORD,
teach me your paths.
—Psalm 25:4

All I was trying to do was fix the sprinklers.

A fairly straightforward plumbing job. The guy who came to drain our system and blow it out for the winter told me last fall that there was a crack in "the main valve," and I'd better replace the thing before I turned the water back on come next summer. For the past several days it had been hot—midnineties, unusually hot for Colorado in May—and I knew I'd better get the water going or my yard would soon go the way of the Gobi Desert. Honestly, I looked forward to the project. Really. I enjoy tackling outside chores for the most part, enjoy the feeling of having triumphed over some small adversity, restoring wellness to my domain. Traces of Adam, I suppose—rule and subdue, be fruitful, all that.

I disengaged the large brass valve from the system on the side of the house, set off to the plumbing store to get a new one. "I need one of these," I said to the guy behind the counter. "It's called a reducing valve," he replied, with a touch of condescension. Okay, so I didn't know that. I'm an amateur. Nevertheless, I'm ready to go. Valve in hand, I returned home to tackle the project. A new challenge loomed before me: soldering a piece of copper pipe to a copper fitting that carried the water from the house to the sprinklers, reduced in pressure by the valve now in my possession. It seemed simple enough. I even followed the instructions that came with the butane torch I bought. (Following instructions is usually something I do only once a project has become a NASCAR pileup, but this was new ground for me, the valve was expensive, and I didn't want to screw the whole thing up.) Sure enough, I couldn't do it, couldn't get the solder to melt into the joint as needed to prevent leaks.

Suddenly, I was angry.

Now, I used to get angry at the drop of a hat, sometimes violently angry as a teen, punching holes in the walls of my bedroom, kicking holes in doors. But the years have had their mellowing effect, and by the grace of God there has also been the sanctifying influence of the Spirit, and my anger surprised me. It felt . . . disproportionate to the issue at hand. I can't get a pipe soldered together. So? *I've never done this before. Cut yourself some slack.* But reason was not exactly ruling the moment, and in anger I stormed into the house to try to find some help.

Like so many men in our culture—solitary men who have no father around to ask how to do this or that, no other men around at all, or too much pride to ask the men who are around—I turned to the Internet, found one of those sites that explains things like how to surmount household plumbing problems, watched a little animated video on how to solder copper pipe. It felt . . . weird. I'm trying to play the man and fix my own sprinklers but I can't and there's no man here to show me how and so I'm watching a cute little video for the mechanically challenged and feeling like about ten years old. A cartoon for a man who is really a boy. Armed with information and wobbling confidence, I go back out, give it another try. Another miss.

At the end of the first round I merely felt like an idiot. Now I feel like an idiot doomed to failure. . . . Now, I do know this—I know that I am not alone in feeling alone. Most of the guys I've ever met feel like this at some point.[1]

⸺⊷⊶⊷⸺

While we all may acknowledge that "yes, I'm on a journey," most of us have some real questions of where this will all end. Will anything change? Will life get better? easier? Will I ever be able to deal well with sprinklers? teenage children? a changing career landscape? Will life be more fulfilling? Will I just live my "threescore and ten" years and die with an ache that tells me I could have done so much more, been so much more? Or will things change, and will I find this "journey" taking me more and more into the man I long to be, the man I dream of being—even the man God has designed me to be? We believe you can.

HOW THIS STUDY WORKS

Through this eight-session DVD series, *Fathered by God*, you'll encounter God in a life-changing way. The design of the Participant's Guide is to facilitate conversation between a small group of men and to provide some direction and questions for going deeper on each topic as an individual between your meeting times.

Before you start, consider the following:

- Start by surrendering yourself to God and his purposes for you in this Participant's Guide. Yield your mind, volition, heart, spirit, soul, and masculinity to God, and simply invite him to do whatever he'd like.

- Commit yourself to the pace God would have you go through the material. Determine to be responsive to his prodding as you may take a little more time on a particular section or question, or take a walk or break and allow for a more natural context for him to speak. A simple way of putting all this is, walk with God.

- Another thought on the pace of this journey: it would be cruel to your heart to skip the times of reading, reflection, and prayer that will make this series all that motivated you to participate in it. Don't fall into the "just get through the material" stride that ends up limiting God and profiting your heart little.

- This series is presented in eight DVD sessions, each about 25 minutes in length. Each session corresponds with topics and material found in the book *Fathered by God*. The series is designed to be used one session at a time, with small groups of men meeting together for an hour and a half each week to view the DVD and discuss the topic. (By the end of the eight weeks, most groups will want to continue with other resources we have available.)

- Each week you should gather at a set time to watch the DVD session together (25 minutes). Read through the "Key Thoughts"

(5 minutes) and discuss the group questions, which focus on the DVD material (50 minutes). End your time with the "Closing Thoughts and Prayer" on the DVD. (The "Going Deeper" section is designed for personal reflection.)

- Each member of the group should commit to coming to the weekly gatherings prepared for discussion—have an open spirit, a vulnerable heart, and a thoughtful mind. To foster a spirit of intimacy in your group, limit your group size to no more than eight people.

You're about to discover a deeper understanding of your true identity in Christ, your original masculinity. It may be challenging at times, and you may want to throw in the towel, but when you finish, you will be confident of your relationship with your Father, God, and you will be more secure than ever in your manhood. Welcome to the journey!

PRAYER

Christ, I come thirsty and hungry for more of you. I yield myself completely and totally to you. I surrender my heart, mind, spirit, and soul to you, inviting you to touch, deliver, speak, heal, counsel, teach, and train me in whatever areas and ways you choose. I give you my expectations for this study. Protect me from the ploys of the evil one, and I stand in your authority against all distractions, impatience, diminishment, self-contempt, lies, deceptions, and temptations to turn to any other god for comfort. Open up the time for reflection, study, and prayer. Guide me through this material. And speak to me in any way you choose. I ask that you use these films and these conversation guides to fill me with your life that I might more fully live in your Larger Story and, with you, rescue the hearts and souls of many. Amen.

THE MASCULINE JOURNEY

*Stand at the crossroads and look; ask for the
ancient paths, ask where the good way is, and
walk in it, and you will find rest for your souls.*

—Jeremiah 6:16

*When I was a child, I talked like a child, I thought
like a child, I reasoned like a child. When I became
a man, I put childish ways behind me.*

—1 Corinthians 13:11

The world in which we live has lost something vital, something core
to understanding life and a man's place in it. For the time in
which we live is a fatherless time. I mean this in two ways.
First, most men and most boys have no real relationship with their earthly fathers, so they have no one
to guide them through the jungles of the masculine

journey. They are—most of us are—unfinished and unfathered men. Or boys. Or boys in men's bodies.

Our way of looking at the world has changed. We no longer live, either as a society or even as the church, with a father-view of the world, a view centered on the presence of a loving and strong father deeply engaged in our lives, to whom we can turn at any time for the guidance, comfort, and provision we need. But this is actually an occasion for hope! Because the life you've known as a man is *not* all there is. There is another way, a path laid down for centuries by men who have gone before us. A marked trail. And there *is* a Father ready to show us that path and help us follow it.

WATCH SESSION 1:
THE MASCULINE JOURNEY

KEY THOUGHTS

This session corresponds with chapters 1 and 2 from *Fathered by God*. The major points of these chapters are summarized here.

⎯∞⎯

- A boy has a lot to learn in his journey to become a man, and he becomes a man only through the active intervention of his father and the fellowship of men.

- Masculinity is bestowed. A boy learns who he is and what he's made of from a man (or a company of men). It can't be learned from other boys, and it can't be learned from the world of women.

- Masculine initiation is a journey; a process; a quest, really; a story that unfolds over time.

- A man's life is a process of initiation into true masculinity. It is a series of stages we soak in and progress through.

- We need more than a moment, a singular celebration, or ritual to take us into manhood. We need a process, a journey, an epic story of many experiences woven together, building upon one another in a progression. We need initiation. And we need a Guide.

- We aren't meant to figure life out on our own. God wants to father us. At any point in a boy's or a man's life, God primarily is initiating him. So much of what we misinterpret as hassles or trials or screwups on our part is, in fact, God giving us experiences to strengthen us, or heal us, or dismantle some unholy thing in us. In other words, to initiate us—a distinctly masculine venture.

DISCUSS

I started the video session talking about trying to repair my '78 Land Cruiser. And in the introduction to this guide, I told the story of looking on the Internet to figure out how to solder the copper pipes for my sprinkler system.

❖ Describe a time when you've felt foolish or as though you were "less of a man."

❖ What about this session on the masculine journey stands out to you? What do you find yourself reacting to most strongly?

What we have now is a world of uninitiated men. Partial men. Boys, mostly, walking around in men's bodies, with men's jobs and families, finances, and responsibilities.[1]

A boy doesn't become a man simply because he gets older. Becoming a man is a process. A boy has a lot to learn in his journey to become a man, and he becomes a man only through the active intervention of his father and the fellowship of men. He needs someone to show him how to throw a fastball, call a girl, and land the job.

❖ Do these realities stir up in you . . .

- Hopelessness?—"I never had that . . . I'll never be the man I want to be," or, "There's no one who can guide me."

- Pride/Arrogance?—"I'm a self-made man who made it because I didn't need anyone else."

- Impatience?—"Journey? Process? Not interested. I'm looking for something quicker."
- Yes!—"A map and a compass. Thank God!"

Most of us fake masculine strength. We present ourselves to the world as having an external masculinity that, internally, we know we don't. Our journey involves coming to the point of admitting that we are unfinished men who need fathering.

❖ Where are you on the continuum of seeing yourself as an unfinished man?

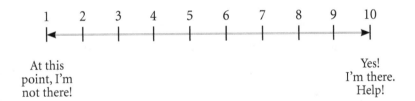

| 1 | 2 | 3 | 4 | 5 | 6 | 7 | 8 | 9 | 10 |

At this
point, I'm
not there!

Yes!
I'm there.
Help!

❖ Say a little more about why you chose that point on the continuum.

❖ Where are you on the continuum of acknowledging you can't do this yourself, that you need someone to guide you?

| 1 | 2 | 3 | 4 | 5 | 6 | 7 | 8 | 9 | 10 |

At this
point, I'm
not there!

Yes!
I'm there.
Help!

❖ Say a little more about why you chose that point on the continuum.

We aren't meant to figure life out on our own. God comes to us as Father. The primary way he presents himself in Scripture is as Father. The truth is, he has been fathering us for a long time—we just haven't had the eyes to see it.

❖ What's your internal reaction to the thought that God wants to father you?

❖ Have you experienced God as a Father? If yes, describe the situation or event.

Most of what God has been trying to do in my life is to come to me as a Father and initiate me. And most of what I've viewed as hassle, trial, or abandonment has actually been occasions where God was either trying to surface an unfathered place in my heart or take me through an experience to provide the fathering I need.

❖ Do any of the following statements describe the way you view the hassles, disappointing people, and challenges of life?

- "I'm just an idiot."
- "God has abandoned me."
- "God is surfacing areas he wants to father me in."
- Or maybe something else: " _____."

❖ What is God currently doing to "initiate" you?

CLOSING THOUGHTS AND PRAYER

Press play on your DVD player. The remaining portion of the video will lead you through a few final thoughts and a prayer.

I will be a Father to you, and you will be my sons.

—2 Corinthians 6:18

GOING DEEPER

If you're truly wanting to embrace the untamed journey Christ has planned for you, you won't be satisfied thinking about this just once a week. This section is designed for you to study the topic further on your own after your group meets. So make some time throughout the week (on your lunch break, instead of watching TV at night, or in the early morning) to read through these questions and consider what God's saying to you here.

The first discussion time can begin slowly and feel awkward. You can be vulnerable and honest with one another, which is initially uncomfortable but ultimately rewarding. Or you fake it, hide, or pose, and who wants to live that life?

◈ How did the group conversation and interaction go this week? Did you find yourself reluctant to share your thoughts? Did you temper them or regret saying too much?

◈ What did God impress you with or say to you as you were meeting with the men?

◈ As a boy or a young man, where did you look for your definition or understanding of masculinity?

◈ How about now?

Life will test you, my brothers. Like a ship at sea, you *will* be tested, and the storms will reveal the weak places in you as a man. They already have. How else do you account for the anger you feel, the fear, the vulnerability to certain temptations? Why can't you marry the girl? Having married, why can't you handle her emotions? Why haven't you found your life's mission? Why do financial crises send you into a rage or depression? You know what I speak of. And so our basic approach to life comes down to this: we stay in what we can handle, and steer clear of everything else. We engage where we feel we can or we must—as at work—and we hold back where we feel sure to fail, as in the deep waters of relating to our wife or our children, and in our spirituality.[2]

Has life tested you? It takes some guts to admit that you fit the descriptor "partial men, boys, mostly, walking around in men's bodies." And yet, if we are honest about how we often feel and view ourselves, it's true, isn't it?

❖ In what "worlds" do you feel like a partial man?

- In your career?

- In the wild?

- In the world of finance, personal budget, money management?

- With a woman?

- As a father?

- In the spiritual world . . . with God?

- With mechanical things?

- In relationships?

- In the arts?

- Other: _____

❖ What specifically makes you feel as though you're lacking in these areas?

❖ How has your journey taken you through those areas in your past and your present? Has God spent time initiating you in those parts of your life?

At any point in a boy's or man's life, God is *primarily* initiating him. So much of what we misinterpret as hassles or trials or screwups on our part is, in fact, God fathering us, taking us through something in order to strengthen us, or heal us, or dismantle some unholy thing in us. This is a distinctly masculine venture.

❖ What hassles, trials, and difficulties might God be currently using to initiate you?

We don't know much about stages of development in our instant culture. But God is a God of *process*. An oak tree starts as an acorn. The Bible was written during a span of more than a thousand years. And a man begins as a boy. Far better for us—and for those who have to live with us, who look up to us—to rediscover the God-ordained stages of masculine development and honor them, live within them, and raise our sons through them.

❖ Does the process involved in the masculine journey encourage or discourage you? Why?

❖ Why is God the only one who can properly father you, properly initiate you?

PRAYER

Spend time with God in prayer, asking him to give you an honest and accurate understanding of the events in your life and his role in them. Welcome him as your Father.

———⸱⸱⸱———

Father, it is you who lures me; it is you who has revealed a greater and deeper need for you; it is you who makes me hunger and thirst for more. I come to you, Father, as an unfinished man. I come needy; I come asking you to make me a whole man, a strong man, an initiated man. I invite you to disrupt, heal, encourage, deliver, convict, and counsel me as you desire. I surrender myself entirely to your fathering of me.

Father, do this for me. Initiate me. I invite you. I give you permission to do whatever you desire that my journey would culminate in my living the full life you have for me as a man. Open my eyes to all you have for me in each of the stages. Come for me, Father, come for me. Amen.

NEXT WEEK

Next week your group will discuss the second DVD segment, "Boyhood." In order to be prepared to share your thoughts with your group, read chapter 3 from *Fathered by God* this week prior to your group meeting.

NOTES

SESSION

2

BOYHOOD

Keep me as the apple of your eye.

—Psalm 17:8

How gladly would I treat you like sons.

—Jeremiah 3:19

We now begin our journey by looking backward, to what our lives as boys were like. More important, we want to examine what they were *meant* to be. So much of the way we approach life as men was set in motion in our youth—some of it for good, and some not so good. We want to recover what was good and find healing for all that was not.

WATCH SESSION 2:
BOYHOOD

KEY THOUGHTS

This session corresponds with chapter 3 from *Fathered by God*. The major points of this chapter are summarized here.

———❦———

- Our worldview as men was set in motion in boyhood.

- Boyhood is a time of exploration and wonder, and to be a boy is to be an explorer. We see this best in the garden of Eden, when life was completely safe and secure yet full of mystery and adventure.

- Each of us is the beloved son, the apple of our Father's eye. You are noticed. Your heart matters. Your Father adores you.

- It is crucial that the beloved son stage (or any of the developmental stages, for that matter) not be cut short, assaulted, unfinished, or stolen in any way.

- We were designed to soak in these stages *for years*, learn their lessons, and have them written indelibly upon our hearts.

DISCUSS

❖ Boyhood is full of adventure and exploration. What is your favorite memory of exploring or adventuring from your childhood?

Recalling your boyhood can raise wonderful memories of innocence, exploration, growth, and wonder. It can also surface some of the most painful events of your life.

❖ As you watched this session on boyhood, where did you find your heart and mind wandering? What stood out to you in this session? Any strong reactions?

When God set Adam in the garden of Eden, he set his son in a world that was, at the very same moment, safe and secure yet full of mystery and adventure. There was no reason whatsoever to be afraid, and every reason to dare. Such is the world God intended for a boy. And like Adam, we are the beloved son, the apple of our Father's eye.

❖ How comfortable are you being referred to as "the beloved son"?

❖ How or when, over the course of your life, has God brought to you a sense that you are his beloved son?

The Father longs for us to know we are his beloved sons. It's a theme of Scripture he drives home through story and teaching. Jesus walked through the world knowing he was the Beloved Son, the favored one. It's what enabled him to live as he did. We were meant to know this too. This relationship was meant to be our secret, our joy also. But there are few who came through their boyhoods with such knowledge intact, without a trace of doubt.

❖ What will have to happen for your position as "beloved son of God" to be the foundation of your identity?

❖ How might that change your life?

❖ What (in a practical sense) does it mean to you to think of God as your Father?

❖ Do you expect God to show up each day as your Father?

Men are reluctant at times to acknowledge that they have been wounded. There's a macho misperception that tells us that admitting to a wound is to somehow admit, in essence, that you're not a man . . . because a real man could never really hurt.

❖ How were you wounded as a boy?

❖ In what ways does your wound continue to define your life?

God is not willing to simply let our woundedness be the end of the story. Not in any man's life. Filled with compassion, our Father God will come as a loving Father and take us close to his heart. He will also take us back to heal the wounds, finish things that didn't get finished. He will come for the boy, no matter how old he might now be, and make him his beloved son.

❖ Can you imagine God coming to heal and restore your soul? To make himself known as your Father? Why or why not?

CLOSING THOUGHTS AND PRAYER

Press play on your DVD player. The remaining portion of the video will lead you through a few final thoughts and a prayer.

Praise the Lord.
How good it is to sing praises to our God,
how pleasant and fitting to praise him! . . .
He heals the brokenhearted
and binds up their wounds.
—Psalm 147:1, 3

GOING DEEPER

Take some time this week to read chapter 3 in *Fathered by God* again and answer these questions on your own after your group meeting.

———∞———

❖ How did the group conversation and interaction go this week? Was it hard to remember your boyhood, or did a lot of memories flood your mind?

❖ What did God impress you with or say to you as you were meeting with the men?

❖ What have you learned about God's plans for you, his design for your life as a man?

The enemy's one central purpose is to separate us from the Father. He uses neglect to whisper, *You see—no one cares. You're not worth caring about.* He uses a sudden loss of innocence to whisper, *This is a dangerous world, and you are alone. You've been abandoned.* He uses assaults and abuses to scream at a boy, *This is all you are good for.* And in this way he makes it nearly impossible for us to know what Jesus knew (that he was God's Beloved Son), makes it so very, very hard to know the Father's heart toward us. The details of each boy's story are unique, but the effect is always a wound in the soul, and with it separation from and suspicion of the Father.

❖ In what way was your boyhood stage cut short? How did that contribute to your wound?

❖ Regardless of the successes or failures of your earthly father, have you found God to truly be a Father to you? Someone who cares and wants to give you good gifts? Be specific.

This is the message of Jesus: There is a good and loving Father who cares deeply and passionately for you. He yearns to be your Father now. He will draw near, if you'll let him. No matter how old you are, your true Father wants you to experience being his beloved son, and all the joys of boyhood that go with it.

❖ Describe a way you might let the joys of boyhood back into your heart.

Being God's beloved son requires that we open our hearts, which will take us back into some of our deepest wounds, into the cynicism and resignation that shut our hearts in the first place.

❖ Why does God require that we open our hearts before he can actively engage us as our Father?

❖ As you finish this chapter, what do you sense God saying to you about being the beloved son? Capture those thoughts now, for they will be quickly forgotten or stolen.

PRAYER

Confess your wounds and ask God to enter your life as a compassionate Father, ready to heal and restore your souls.

—⊗⊗⊗—

Father, what did I miss here, in this stage? Did I know I was the beloved son? Do I believe it even now? Come to me, in this place, over these years. Speak to me. Do I believe you want good things for me? Is my heart secure in your love? How was my young heart wounded in my life as a boy? And Jesus, you who came to heal the broken heart, come to me here. Heal this stage in my heart. Restore me as the beloved son. Father me. Amen.

NEXT WEEK

Next week your group will discuss the third DVD segment, "Cowboy." In order to be prepared to share your thoughts with your group, read chapter 4 from *Fathered by God* this week prior to your group meeting.

NOTES

SESSION

COWBOY

And [the boy] grew in wisdom and stature,
and in favor with God and men.

—Luke 2:52

Be men of courage; be strong.

—1 Corinthians 16:13

Men, and boys, learn by doing; we learn through experience. It's one thing to be *told* you have what it takes. It's another thing altogether to *discover* that you have what it takes, through some trial brought up in an adventure or through some test that hard work demands. For masculine initiation is not a spectator sport. It is something that must be *entered into*. It is one part instruction and nine parts experience.

WATCH SESSION 3:
COWBOY

KEY THOUGHTS

This session corresponds with chapter 4 from *Fathered by God*. The major points of this chapter are summarized here.

⸻

- The cowboy (or ranger) stage begins in early adolescence—around age twelve or thirteen—and carries into the midtwenties.

- A notable shift takes place in a boy's soul as he approaches his teens—a yearning for real adventure. Something inside tells him that he needs to prove himself, needs to be tested.

- It is at this age that a boy begins to ask himself, "Do I have what it takes?" In the cowboy stage the answer comes partly through adventure, and partly through hard work.

- Men, and boys, learn by doing; we learn through experience. The experience is both a revelation and a kind of authoring, in that it reveals to you what you are made of and writes the lesson on your heart.

- When he reaches the cowboy stage, a young man needs to know that life is hard. If he doesn't learn this, he will use all his energy trying to make life comfortable, soft, and nice, and that is no way for any man to spend his life.

- The cowboy heart is wounded in a young man if he is never allowed to have adventure, and it is wounded if he has no one to take him there. It is wounded if he has no confidence-building experiences with work. And it is wounded if the adventure or the work is overwhelming, unfit to the heart of the boy, or if he repeatedly fails there.

DISCUSS

❖ Boys need to experience hard physical work to answer the Question, "Do I have what it takes?" What was the first job you had as a kid? How did you feel about it?

❖ What's your immediate reaction to this DVD session? Who or what spoke to your heart?

My childhood summers were spent in eastern Oregon on my grandparents' ranch. When I was about thirteen years old, a steer had gotten loose on his property, and it was one of the defining moments of my cowboy stage when my grandfather told me to go take care of it, clearly indicating that he wouldn't be coming to help me. It was an event that gave me the confidence that I do have what it takes.

❖ What have been the memorable "adventures" or "hard work" experiences of your life that required more of you than you realized you had? Were there elements of anxiety, fear, or apprehension involved? How did things turn out?

In the cowboy stage we choose to pursue adventure or hard work, and often that becomes the defining story of our lives. It is through that outlet that we answer the Question every man asks: Do I have what it takes? And until we receive God's answer, we are driven to find it somewhere.

❖ Where do you go for your answer to the Question, "Do I have what it takes?" Work, adventure, a woman?

Several times I use the illustration of David as a young man who was tested in the field with both adventure and hard work. These were the experiences that gave him confidence for a bigger adventure in his battle with Goliath, a classic story.

❖ Were you prepared for the battles you have faced in life?

❖ How was your cowboy heart wounded? Was your cowboy stage cut short? If so, how?

Teddy Roosevelt was an unfinished man who sought out experiences that would validate his masculinity. Knowing that his youth had been too limited in experience, he put himself into the "field" for the adventures and hard work he needed to develop his unfathered heart.

❖ What adventures or hard work could you imagine putting yourself into for the fathering of your heart?

Others, like Morgan in his story of getting lost on his hunting trip, experience adventure or hard work even when they don't seek it out. Morgan felt that God told him he'd arranged his getting lost to teach him that he did his best and that he does have what it takes, even though accusations told him he was a failure.

❖ Have you asked God if you have what it takes?

❖ Has he answered you? How?

If you weren't the beloved son, the testing that comes with this stage can feel unkind, cruel, a sort of rejection—especially if you are on your own. . . .

The masculine soul needs the trials and adventures and experiences that bring a young man to the *settled confidence* David showed before Goliath—the lion and the bear experiences. All of these experiences of the cowboy stage are driving at one basic goal: to answer his Question. The boy-becoming-a-young-man has a Question, and the Question is, "Do I have what it takes?"[1]

❖ How would you love to hear God answer your Question?

CLOSING THOUGHTS AND PRAYER

Press play on your DVD player. The remaining portion of the video will lead you through a few final thoughts and a prayer.

Your servant has killed both the lion and the bear; this uncircumcised Philistine will be like one of them, because he has defied the armies of the living God. The LORD who delivered me from the paw of the lion and the paw of the bear will deliver me from the hand of this Philistine.

—1 Samuel 17:36–37

GOING DEEPER

Before answering these questions alone, read and reflect more on the cowboy in chapter 4 of *Fathered by God.*

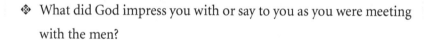

❖ What did God impress you with or say to you as you were meeting with the men?

❖ Having read the chapter on the cowboy, what jumped out at you that didn't in the DVD segment?

❖ How has experience, testing, trials, or adventures answered your Question, "Do I have what it takes?"

David was barely a teen when he offered to fight the giant. And when the king attempted to dissuade him, he argued his competence confidently (1 Samuel 17:33–37). Being a shepherd was David's cowboy stage, and he learned lessons then that would carry him the rest of his life. There was a settled confidence in the boy—he knew he had what it took. But he also knew that God had been with him.

❖ Are you open to the idea that God might call you to do great and dangerous things, as he did David?

❖ If God did call you to a wild adventure, do you believe you'd be able to do what he asked of you?

❖ If you are hearing these messages, where do you think they are coming from?

❖ What needs to happen in your life so that, as David did, you can step into the epic story God has for you?

While the cowboy stage is a time of great adventure, it's equally a time of learning to work. David's years spent as a shepherd were *hard work*. Jesus worked in the carpenter's shop, and that is significant. Working with wood and tools, side by side with your father, does things for a young man that few other situations offer.

❖ Did you have models of men who worked hard when you were growing up? If so, who were they and what did they do?

❖ What did you learn about life from their work ethic?

❖ Do you have a good work ethic, or have you struggled when it comes to hard physical work? What impact has this had on you?

❖ Boys need adventure and hard work, and they need someone to let them experience it, to teach them on their journey. Was your cowboy stage cut short by a parent who wouldn't allow you to risk adventure or hard work as a teenager? If so, what was the impact of this on you?

❖ If not, who guided you on this journey, and what did you learn from their teaching?

❖ What was God's main message to you during your cowboy stage?

PRAYER

The Question has been stirred up in our soul this week. If you haven't already, it's time to take it before God and seek out his answer.

Father, take me back, back to the cowboy stage, and finish the unfinished business I need here in my soul as a man. Heal the wounded cowboy in me. Take me into adventure and danger and hard work—simple work. Take me into the shop and into the field, to the places where the soul of a young man is made strong. Father me here. And give me the grace to father my sons, and the young men around me, as true cowboys. Help me to initiate them, even as you are initiating me. Amen.

NEXT WEEK

Next week your group will discuss the fourth DVD segment, "Warrior." In order to be prepared to share your thoughts with your group, read chapter 5 from *Fathered by God* this week prior to your group meeting.

SESSION

WARRIOR

It is God who arms me with strength . . .
He makes my feet like the feet of a deer;
he enables me to stand on the heights.
He trains my hands for battle.

—Psalm 18:32–34

Gird your sword upon your side, O mighty one.

—Psalm 45:3

Historian Thomas Cahill, speaking of the violent origin of the Jewish festival of Hanukkah, observed that "there are humiliations a proud people—even one oppressed for generations—cannot abide." Indeed. It may take time, and require repeated provocation, but eventually a man must come to realize that there are certain things in life worth fighting for. Perhaps, when we appreciate the truth of this, we can better understand the heart of God.

Like the Jews before Christ, we, too, live in a world at war. We are supposed to fight back. It is apparently a difficult reality to embrace, as witnessed by the passivity that marks much of modern Christianity. We just want the Christian life to be all about the sweet love of Jesus. But that is not what's going on here. You may not like the situation, but that only makes it unattractive—it does not make it untrue.

WATCH SESSION 4:
WARRIOR

KEY THOUGHTS

This session corresponds with chapter 5 from *Fathered by God*. The major points of this chapter are summarized here.

—∞∞∞—

- Our God is a warrior, mighty and terrible in battle, and he leads armies. It is this God in whose image man is made.

- Our God is a warrior because there are certain things in life worth fighting for, certain things that must be fought for. He makes man a warrior in his own image, because he intends for man to join him in that battle.

- We live in a world at war. We are supposed to fight back.

- The heart of the warrior says, "I will not let evil have its way. There are some things that cannot be endured. I've got to do something. There is freedom to be had." The heart of the warrior says, "I will put myself on the line for you."

- Above all, the warrior learns to yield his heart to nothing. Not to kill his heart for fear of falling into temptation, but to protect his heart for nobler things, to keep the integrity of his heart as a great reservoir of passionate strength and holy desire.

- The warrior heart has been wounded and must be healed if we're to discover our true, masculine heart.

- We have a Father who is a great warrior, and he will raise us as warriors, if we'll let him, if we will embrace the initiation that comes with this stage. There is a warrior in you, by the way.

- God raises the warrior through hardship. What better way to train a warrior than by putting a man in situation after situation where he must fight?

DISCUSS

Most boys grow up with an innate desire to fight. Even if your parents didn't buy you toy guns or swords, you probably figured out how to make pretend weapons from paper towel rolls or simply by using your hand as a gun.

❖ What was your favorite warrior toy as a child?

❖ As you watched this DVD session, what did God stir up in you?

❖ Did you ever get into a fight as a young boy? Who did you fight, and what were the issues you were fighting over? How'd you do in the fight?

Read Exodus 15:3; Psalm 24:7–8; Jeremiah 20:11; and John 2:13–17. The Old Testament writers continually paint the picture of God as a warrior; and John shares the story of Jesus so outraged that, in an act of premeditated aggression, he sat down, built for himself a whip of cords, and used it on the merchants occupying the temple courtyards.

❖ Is this the kind of behavior you'd expect from the Jesus you've been told about?

In the video, Bart told the story of calling out a guy who had flipped him off. As a young man, he was riding his bike when five guys drove by in their car and one of them flipped Bart off. Bart confronted them and all of them leaped out of the car and beat the heck out of Bart. Bart felt such shame and humiliation for trying to fight and it not going well. Bart connected this event with his Question, comparing himself to his warrior dad and wondering if, when the battle gets fierce, does he have what it takes?

❖ What in Bart's story struck you?

❖ When, where, and over what have you tried to fight and it didn't go well?

Our God is a warrior because there are certain things in life worth fighting for, that must be fought for. He makes man a warrior in his own image, because he intends for man to join him in that battle.

❖ In which of these areas do you see yourself as being in a war/battle?

- Your marriage?
- Your children?
- Relationships?
- Your church?
- Those you work for or with?
- Other: _____

The tendency is for us to be either passive and disengaged, or to be driven, always in "attack mode" (which is not the same as courage). My story of literally running away from the opportunity to confront my boss about his poor leadership is probably painfully familiar to many of you. Craig admits his tendency to be passive, while Morgan, not knowing how to say no, takes on every battle that makes itself available to him. The warrior in each of us ends up being taken out . . . to the enemy's delight.

❖ Is your tendency to be passive or driven? Describe.

❖ Do you feel you need to change your tendencies, or are you content with your current situation?

I commented about our being "thrown" by the way God trains and raises up a warrior. God puts us into battle; he allows and even arranges for trials, obstacles, and hassles to come into our lives so that we have to face them. He's not being cruel; he's actually developing us, training us . . . fathering us as warriors. He's saying, "It's time, my son. You must rise up."

❖ What is God bringing into your life for your rising up and being further trained as a warrior?

There is hope for each of us in recovering our warrior heart. Jesus no longer had Joseph around when he entered his warrior stage. On a human level, he was fatherless. But we know he was not alone. We, too, have a Father who is a great Warrior, and he will raise us as warriors, if we'll let him, if we will embrace the initiation that comes with this stage. However it has been handled up to this point in your life, the warrior in you can be restored, recovered, and made strong.

❖ What do you long for God to say to you about your warrior heart?

CLOSING THOUGHTS AND PRAYER

Press play on your DVD player. The remaining portion of the video will lead you through a few final thoughts and a prayer.

The LORD will march out like a mighty man, like a
warrior he will stir up his zeal; with a shout he will raise
the battle cry and will triumph over his enemies.

—Isaiah 42:13

GOING DEEPER

Spend some time this week reading chapter 5 in *Fathered by God*
again, and answering these questions alone after your group discussion.

❖ What does God's being a warrior evoke in you? Is it comforting or
disturbing? Why or why not?

◈ What picture of Christ did you have growing up? Or even now?

- Christ as a gentle shepherd with a young lamb draped over his shoulders?
- The masculine carpenter with the warm, broad smile?
- Mr. Rogers with a beard?
- A skilled and fierce warrior?
- Other: _____

The heart of the warrior is wounded in a boy and in a young man when he is told that aggression is flat-out wrong or unchristian, that niceness equals godliness, or when his attempts to rise up as a warrior are mocked or crushed. He is wounded when he has no one to train him.

◈ In what ways have you been wounded as a warrior?

Adam was created to act, endowed with the image of a mighty God who acts and intervenes dramatically. In the Garden, Adam failed by not engaging; and therefore paralysis—another word for passivity— became one of the many things the first man passed on to the rest of us men.

❖ In what ways are you disengaged and passive like Adam?

Many of us have been taught to ignore the devil, that resisting him is God's work. That is dangerous thinking, and unbiblical.

"Resist the devil" (James 4:7).

"Resist him" (1 Peter 5:9).

We live in a world at war. We are supposed to fight back. It is apparently a difficult reality to embrace, as witnessed by the passivity that marks much of modern Christianity. You may not like the situation, but that only makes it *unattractive*—it does not make it *untrue*.

❖ What is currently happening in your life and relationships that may be an assault of the enemy that you now need to resist?

PRAYER

Spend some time in prayer, asking God to heal and guide your warrior heart—that you will pick your battles wisely and fight with strength and valor.

⎯⎯⎯∞⎯⎯⎯

Father, show me where I have lost heart as a warrior. What did I miss here? What was wounded, and what was surrendered? Take me back to those times and places when the warrior in me was shut down. Wake the warrior heart in me. Train me. Show me what I have surrendered, where I am walking in passivity. Teach me an unyielding heart. Rouse me. I am willing. I am yours. And help me to raise my sons and the young men around me to be warriors in your image. Show me where the warrior is emerging in them, how to strengthen it, call it forth, and make it holy. Amen.

NEXT WEEK

Next week your group will discuss the fifth DVD segment, "Lover." In order to be prepared to share your thoughts with your group, read chapter 6 from *Fathered by God* this week prior to your group meeting.

NOTES

SESSION

LOVER

I found the one my heart loves.

—Song of Songs 3:4

One thing I ask of the LORD,
this is what I seek:
that I may dwell in the house of the LORD
all the days of my life,
to gaze upon the beauty of the LORD
and to seek him in his temple.

—Psalm 27:4

Now we come to a fork in the road in the masculine journey, a stage that is both essential and, sadly, often overlooked and bypassed by many men. It is the lover stage. By this I do not primarily mean that time in a young man's life when he falls in love with a girl. Though that is part of it, I don't believe it is the core of the stage or even its ultimate expression. Instead, this is the season in a man's life when his masculine

heart is awakened to beauty and ultimately "The Beauty" when he discovers a sacred romance with God.

WATCH SESSION 5:
LOVER

KEY THOUGHTS

This session corresponds with chapter 6 from *Fathered by God*. The major points of this chapter are summarized here.

—⚬⚬⚬—

- If the evil one cannot take the warrior out, cannot keep him from entering the battle at all, as he has intimidated so many men, he will try to overwhelm him with too many battles instead.

- Down through its history the church has held up the good, the true, and the beautiful as a sort of trinity of virtues.

- This trinity matches the stages of the masculine journey: the boy begins to understand Good as he learns right from wrong; the warrior fights for what is True; and a man comes to see that Beauty is the best of the three when the lover is awakened.

- It is very good for the warrior to be arrested by Beauty. It provides a great balance to his soul, so he is more than simply a fighter.

- That which draws us to the heart of God is often that which first lifts our own hearts above the mundane. And the life of your heart is what God is most keenly pursuing.

- The danger for the warrior is that life becomes defined by battle, and that is not good for the soul nor true to our story. There is something deeper than battle, and that is Romance.

- While in other stages God is our Father and Initiator, when the lover stage emerges, God invites the man to become his "intimate one." This is a crucial stage.

- This awakening of his heart is essential for a man to truly love a woman.

- The heart of the lover never gets to awaken or develop in a man as long as he chooses to remain in the world of analysis, dissection, and "reason is everything." He must heed his emotions, his heart.

DISCUSS

❖ There is a moment in every man's life when he abandons his boyhood by recognizing beauty. Who was the girl who opened your eyes to the fact that there is romance and beauty in life? Was it your first-grade classmate, or the woman you're married to now, or someone in between?

❖ What's your immediate reaction to this DVD session? Who or what spoke to your heart?

❖ What are the most beautiful places you've ever visited? You may not be a poet, but do your best to describe them.

In the video, I share about the death of my best friend in a climbing accident eleven years ago and the shattering grief I felt. I couldn't pray; I couldn't read my Bible. The only thing that seemed to help was beauty. I found that long walks in the mountains were a source of comfort, solace in a season of grief and pain. It was in and through beauty that I found the presence of God, something akin to what David describes in Psalm 23:2–3.

❖ Have you had a similar experience in life, where a sunset, a stream, a garden, or clouds brought hope, life, and comfort? Is there a time when beauty brought God to your heart?

❖ When was your heart first awakened to beauty? Describe the experience.

David was a rugged adventurer, a warrior. But he was also a musician, a poet, and a man with a heart that was alive to God. This is crucial to point out because most men hide in reason, logic, and analysis. Yet the Scriptures make clear that the heart is central to your being—from it flow the springs of life (Proverbs 4:23)!

❖ When it comes to your masculine makeup, are you more engineer or poet? Do you hide behind reason and logic, as many men do, or do you feel free to embrace beauty?

Most men relate to Eve either as "consumers" (looking to get something from a woman) or as "lovers" (offering strength and love to a woman).

❖ Which most accurately describes your motives in relating to woman—"lover" or "consumer"?

There are many reasons why a man may shy away from his heart. He may have been shamed, or he may have simply never been invited to explore his heart. But we must remember that the lover is wounded in a man (often starting in his youth) when he looks to a woman for the primary love and validation his father was meant to bestow. Through this relationship with the woman, he suffers a wound.

❖ How was your heart wounded in your development as a lover?

It's at the lover stage that a man's relationship with God opens to a new frontier. God has invited man into an intimate relationship. As Chesterton reminded us, "Romance is the deepest thing in life." Ours is a love story. Anything short of it is a Christianity of dry bones.

❖ How comfortable are you with language referring to our Lord as our lover? Is this foreign to you? Is it awkward?

❖ Do you wish for an intimate relationship with God, or do you feel hesitation in that? Explain.

CLOSING THOUGHTS AND PRAYER

Press play on your DVD player. The remaining portion of the video will lead you through a few final thoughts and a prayer.

Because your love is better than life, my lips will glorify you.

—Psalm 63:3

GOING DEEPER

As you spend some time in personal reflection, read through chapter 6 again from *Fathered by God*. God will speak and show himself to you as your lover in a variety of ways from this point on. Some of those ways may be huge; others may be little signs or gifts that will expose his heart for you. Keep your eyes, ears, and heart open.

❖ How has God revealed himself to you as a lover this week?

❖ Where and how do you find the beauty your heart needs?

As we've discussed, a boy must go through several stages before he becomes a man. And it's best for a boy-becoming-a-man to complete some of these stages before Eve enters the picture. He needs to understand that he is loved and that he has what it takes before he can properly love a woman.

❖ Did Eve enter your life too early? Were you ready to appreciate her and love her when she presented herself to you?

❖ Why is it so common for men to make Eve the center of their universe?

❖ What, for you, is risky about loving a woman?

David would have had no problem at all understanding this. The poetry that flowed from the heart of this passionate lover is filled with unapologetic emotion toward God. (Read Psalms 4:7; 16:11; 36:8; and 42:1–2.) These are not the words of a dry theologian or moralist. These are not the words of even your average pastor. David is captivated by the beauty he finds in God. The man is undone. He is as smitten as any lover might be, only—can we begin to accept this? do we even have a category for it?—his lover is God.

❖ Have you ever felt you were in love with Christ? Do you know someone who truly has an intimate relationship with Christ?

❖ Describe the relationship you would like to have with God. Ask him for it.

PRAYER

Surrender to God, inviting him to make himself known as your lover.

———— ❧ ————

Father, God, awaken the lover in me. Stir my heart. Romance me. Take me back into the story of love in my life, and show me where I lost heart. Show me where I have chosen safety over coming alive. Show me where deep repentance needs to take place. Heal the lover heart in me. Awaken me.

Lord, open my eyes, give me sight, show me, capture me, allure and entice me with your beauty. May I know that, indeed, your love is better than the love of any woman, better than life itself. Amen.

NEXT WEEK

Next week your group will discuss the sixth DVD segment, "King." In order to be prepared to share your thoughts with your group, read chapter 7 from *Fathered by God* this week prior to your group meeting.

NOTES

SESSION

KING

The highest heavens belong to the LORD,
but the earth he has given to man.

—Psalm 115:16

Well done, good and faithful servant! You have been
faithful with a few things; I will put you in charge of
many things. Come and share your master's happiness!

—Matthew 25:23

We come now to the "goal" of the masculine journey, the maturity for which God has been fathering the man since his first breath—to be a king. It is a man's destiny to wield power, influence, and property in God's name. It is as great and noble an undertaking as it is difficult; history makes that very clear. The reason behind many of our miseries upon the earth in these days is that we have lost our kings.

WATCH SESSION 6:
KING

KEY THOUGHTS

This session corresponds with chapter 7 from *Fathered by God*. The major points of this chapter are summarized here.

——⚬✖⚬——

- The goal of the masculine journey, the maturity for which God has been fathering the man since his first breath, is to be a king—to wield power, influence, and property in his name.

- Before a man is ready to handle power, his character must be forged. It might be said that all masculine initiation is designed to prepare a man to handle power.

- The great problem of the earth and the great aim of the masculine journey boil down to this: when can you trust a man with power?

- As Dallas Willard once said, the whole history of God and man recounted in the Bible is the story of God wanting to entrust men with power, and men not being able to handle it.

- A good king uses all he has to make his kingdom like the kingdom of heaven. We are given power and resources and influence for the benefit of others.

- The true test of a king is this: what is life like for the people under his authority?

- A good king brings order to the realm.

- A good king also fights for the security of his kingdom, battling assault from without and sedition from within. That's why he must be a warrior first.

DISCUSS

Think about your favorite adventure stories or fantasy movies in which a king plays a major role—stories about Camelot, plays by Shakespeare, movies like *Lord of the Rings: Return of the King*, or even the epic poem *Beowulf.*

❖ What fictional or historical king is your favorite, and why?

❖ What's your first reaction to this DVD session on the king?

❖ Imagine yourself as a king in the traditional, romanticized version. Picture your kingdom and the essence of your reign. Now think of your current "kingdom." What words best describe the type of king you'd like to be?

In Genesis 1:26, God describes his purpose for making man. His priorities were to make man 1) in his image and 2) to have dominion in the earth. So, we can understand that the goal of the masculine journey is to rule well, to be good kings.

❖ Up to this point in the study, what have you understood to be the goal of your masculine journey?

As a boy, you are shaped by the kind of king you are raised under. It may be a good king, a loving father whose goal is to show you that you are loved unconditionally. Or it may have been a bad king, a man who took pleasure in your pain. Or it may have been an absent king, who wounded you by not being part of your life.

❖ How were you wounded on your journey to becoming a king? And what are the risks of becoming a king without completing the other stages of the masculine journey?

❖ Think of the kings whose authority you've lived under. Knowing that the test of a good king is how good life is for his subjects, describe how the kings in your life have shaped your desires to be a king. What influence have they had on the type of king you are or want to be?

The great problem of the earth and the great aim of the masculine journey boil down to this: when can you trust a man with power? The annals of the kings are, for the most part, a very sad record. Moses, David, Charlemagne, Lincoln—good kings like that are hard to come by. But my sincere hope is that as we embrace the masculine journey, submit to its lessons, and learn again how to initiate men, we shall make good kings available once more.

❖ Can God entrust you with greater measures of his power at present? If so, to do what?

❖ If not, what must change before he can?

Too many men, having reached the king stage in their lives without first taking the masculine journey, seize the opportunity to make life good . . . *for themselves.* They believe, *Hey—I've paid my dues. Now it's my turn to have some fun.*

❖ Is a self-centered life of comfort, leisure, and fun the life you want to be living now or in your later years?

It is a matter of the heart, my brothers. There are many offices a man might fulfill as a king—head of a household, manager of a department, pastor of a church, coach of a team, prime minister of a nation—but the *heart* required is the same. "The king's heart is in the hand of the LORD; he directs it like a watercourse wherever he pleases" (Proverbs 21:1).

❖ As a king, how do you balance your thirst for adventure and the battle to fight with your responsibilities for those living under your authority?

❖ What has been your biggest test as a king?

Read Joshua 24:15. God is after a man so *yielded* to him, so completely surrendered, that his heart is moved easily by the Spirit of God to the purposes of God.

❖ Reflecting on this verse, do you believe your heart is that of a good king? What could you do to improve life for those living under you?

CLOSING THOUGHTS AND PRAYER

Press play on your DVD player. The remaining portion of the video will lead you through a few final thoughts and a prayer.

Your Father has been pleased to give you the kingdom.

—Luke 12:32

GOING DEEPER

Read through chapter 7 from *Fathered by God* again this week as you reflect on these questions after your group meeting.

❖ What is life like for the people under your authority?

❖ What would your wife say? (Consider asking her.) Do you think she feels stressed, pressured, manipulated, or fearful of your reactions? Does she feel dismissed or overlooked?

❖ What would your children say? (Consider asking them in an appropriate way.) Do you spend most of your energy getting your children to behave as you'd like, or do you look at them individually, trying to understand their hearts and look for ways to bless them?

Before a man is ready to handle power, his character must be forged. It might be said that all masculine initiation is designed to prepare a man to handle power.

❖ In what way do you believe you were initiated to handle power?

❖ Do you feel you passed that initiation, or did you fail to recognize God's hand in preparing you for your current situation?

A good king brings order to his realm. God brings order out of chaos at the beginning of creation, and then he hands the project over to Adam to rule in the same way—not as a tyrant or micromanager. Adam does not have to fear, because God offers his strength to bring order to the realm.

❖ Where is there chaos or a need for well-being in your realm?

❖ What's your plan to restore order?

There is a cost that comes with being king, unknown and unmatched by any other man. You should approach the throne with a profound reluctance. Becoming a king is something we accept only as an act of obedience. The posture of the heart in a mature man is hesitancy in taking the throne but willingness to do it on behalf of others.

❖ Is there a part of your life in which you're hesitant to be the king God has called you to be? If so, why?

PRAYER

A good king recognizes that his power comes only from God, and so he goes to God daily to seek his will. Do that today as you pray.

———⁂———

Father, it is with some hesitation that I ask this—but still, I ask that you come and take me into this stage, initiate me here, when the time is right for me. Show me how the king was wounded in me as a boy, as a young man, and in my adulthood as well. Show me where I've acted weakly, abdicating my authority. Show me where I've been a tyrant. Show me also where I have ruled well. Let me see what life is like for those under my rule, and, by your grace, let me become a great king on behalf of others. I give my life to you. Give me the heart and spirit of a man yielded to you. Father me. Amen.

NEXT WEEK

Next week your group will discuss the seventh DVD segment, "Sage." In order to be prepared to share your thoughts with your group, read chapter 8 from *Fathered by God* this week prior to your group meeting.

SESSION

7

SAGE

The glory of young men is their strength,
gray hair the splendor of the old.
—Proverbs 20:29

The teaching of the wise is a fountain of life,
turning a man from the snares of death.
—Proverbs 13:14

This is the final stage, the crescendo of a man's life. This is the time of wisdom and fathering others, counseling others: Scripture calls it the "elder at the gates." This can be a difficult time because it can feel as though your kingdom is shrinking, but in fact this is the time of your greatest influence. Your life experience is flowing over into the world, shaping the lives of young kings coming up in your steps.

WATCH SESSION 7:
SAGE

KEY THOUGHTS

This session corresponds with chapter 8 from *Fathered by God*. The major points of this chapter are summarized here.

———◦◦◦———

• Too many men are far too willing to offer their thoughts on subjects in which they have no real personal experience—especially experiences of God—and their "wisdom" is not grounded in reality. It is theory, at best, more likely speculation, untested and unproven.

• The stage of the sage begins in the waning years of the king, sometime between the ages of sixty and seventy.

• A sage differs from an expert the way a lover differs from an engineer. To begin with, expertise quite often has nothing to do with walking with God; it may, in fact, lead us farther from him. For the expertise of the specialist gives us the settled assurance that he has matters under control and that we will also, as soon as we put our trust in him.

• On the other hand, the sage communes with God—an existence entirely different from and utterly superior to the life of the expert. Whatever counsel he offers, he draws you to God, not to self-reliance.

• The sage has learned to not lean upon his wisdom, knowing that frequently God is asking things of us that seem counterintuitive, and thus his wisdom (and expertise) are fully submitted to his God.

• Humility is the great dividing line between the expert and the sage, for the sage isn't aware of what he is.

> • The heart of a sage goes undeveloped when a man has been a fool for most of his life, either refusing to take the journey or refusing to take note of the journey he has taken.

DISCUSS

The image of the wise, older man is iconic in our culture and in many others. From the Norman Rockwell paintings of the grandfatherly figure with the young boy to Chinese emphasis on respect for elders, we acknowledge the wisdom of the sage in many ways.

❖ Who has been a sage in your life, imparting wisdom and encouragement learned through experience?

❖ What did this chapter on the sage stir up in you? Longing, disappointments, questions, hopes?

❖ Do you find yourself yearning for a sage? In what area of life would he be most helpful?

- In your marriage?
- In your parenting?
- In your walk with God?
- In your relationships?
- With your finances?
- With issues of health and lifestyle?
- Other: _____

❖ Who could you imagine yourself approaching for counsel, advice, and input regarding your life?

❖ What impact have sages had upon your life? How do you think your life might have been different if a sage had not shared his wisdom with you?

The sage communes with God. He has learned to not lean upon his knowledge, knowing that often God is asking things of us that seem counterintuitive, and thus his expertise must be fully submitted to his God.

❖ To what degree does a desire for self-reliance and expertise keep you from following a God who may ask you to do things counter-intuitive to your instincts and goals?

A sage does not have to be heard, as a warrior might. He does not have to rule, as a king might. There is room in his presence for who you are and where you are. There is understanding. He has no agenda and nothing to lose. What he offers, he offers with kindness and discretion, knowing by instinct those who have ears to hear and those who don't. Thus his words are offered in the right measure, at the right time, to the right person. He will not trouble you with things you do not need to know, nor burden you with things that are not yet yours to bear, nor embarrass you with exposure for shortcomings you are not yet ready to overcome, even though he sees all of that.

❖ Which of these qualities do you think you have at this point in your life?

❖ What will it take for you to become such a man?

❖ Is becoming a sage something you look forward to? Why or why not?

SESSION 7

CLOSING THOUGHTS AND PRAYER

Press play on your DVD player. The remaining portion of the video will lead you through a few final thoughts and a prayer.

Listen, my son, accept what I say,

and the years of your life will be many.

I guide you in the way of wisdom

and lead you along straight paths.

—Proverbs 4:10–11

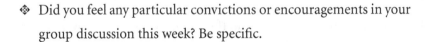

GOING DEEPER

For more on the sage, read chapter 8 of *Fathered by God* and answer the following questions after your group discussion.

❖ Did you feel any particular convictions or encouragements in your group discussion this week? Be specific.

❖ Becoming a sage requires humility to accept that time and experience will teach you things books cannot. Do you accept that?

❖ Are your aspirations to be an expert or a sage? What is the evidence of this in your life now?

❖ Is there someone you spend time with who leaves you with a hunger for more of God? Explain.

❖ What are the questions or issues you'd love to bring to a sage and simply sit at his feet to listen and converse?

- In your marriage?

- In your parenting?

- In your walk with God?

- With your finances?

- With issues of health and lifestyle?

- Other:

If you're a younger man, you're probably recognizing that many of these characteristics of the sage aren't yet present in your life. Don't worry. As you pursue your masculine journey, it will come in due time. For now, commit yourself to take as few shortcuts as possible. Learn your lessons. Take note of all that God is teaching you. Submit to the journey. Be a student of the Scriptures. Hang out with the wise, living or dead, for that is how we, too, become wise.

❖ React to these statements.

If you're older and the sage has gone undeveloped in you, well, you'd better get busy, 'cause time's a-wastin'. At this point you haven't years to go back and gather many experiences; you had best walk closely with God, let him focus you on what he'd have you learn *now*. Some of you just need to be a beloved son. Or perhaps a lover. The wisest thing to do is to seek communion with God.

❖ React to these statements. Can you identify the stage at which you were cut short—the phase of masculine development you weren't allowed to complete? Return there to invite God in for healing.

The boy knows God as Father, the cowboy knows God as the One who initiates, the warrior knows God as the King he serves, the lover knows God as his intimate One, and the king knows God as his trusted Friend. The sage has a deep *communion* with God.

❖ Which of these characteristics of God are you most comfortable with? Which makes the most sense to you?

PRAYER

We start our journeys with the impulsive neediness of boyhood, and we hope to end with the quiet wisdom of a sage. It is a slow process, one that takes years. As you pray today, ask God to place you firmly on the path to becoming a wise man.

———⊶⊷———

Father, I need you now, need you to the end of my days. I ask you to raise the sage in me. Help me to become a man of genuine wisdom and compassion. [For younger men:] Show me the sages you have for me, both living and dead. Help me find them, and allow me to sit at their feet. [For older men:] Show me the men who need my counsel, and show me how to pursue them.

Speak to me, Father; stir the fire in my heart. Show me what my contribution is now to be, and father me in making it with all my heart. Amen.

NEXT WEEK

Next week your group will discuss the seventh DVD segment, "Let Us Be Intentional." In order to be prepared to share your thoughts with your group, read chapter 9 from *Fathered by God* this week prior to your group meeting.

LET US BE INTENTIONAL

You have made known to me the path of life.

—Psalm 16:11

So I say to you: Ask and it will be given to you; seek and you will find; knock and the door will be opened to you.

—Luke 11:9

Over the course of this DVD series, you've heard me mention that you are prized by God, that you are his delight! Jesus addressed this directly in asking the question, "Which of you, if his son asks for bread, will give him a stone?" (Matthew 7:9). In other words, if we, as human fathers have some natural inclination of generosity toward our own sons, how much more is your heavenly Father's love for you? You are prized by God. He longs to be generous toward you!

WATCH SESSION 8:
LET US BE INTENTIONAL

KEY THOUGHTS

This session corresponds with chapter 9 of *Fathered by God*. The major points of this chapter are summarized here.

———

- Jesus enjoyed a relationship with his Father that we also crave. They were close, so close that they were One. We were made for the very same thing, and our lives just aren't right until we have it.

- The victories we treasure are from the hardest battles we've fought. God is treating us with respect, treating us like men. He has something for us in the difficulty. We need to find out what that is, and be shaped and strengthened by it.

- God wants us to be engaged in the process of becoming men—he wants us to be intentional. Our journey of masculine initiation isn't a spectator sport!

- The enemy is a thief, and you must understand—if you have not already noticed this—that his greatest target is simply your joy.

DISCUSS

❖ You've been in this study for eight weeks now, sharing your journey with a group of men. What has been the most interesting thing
about this process for you?

❖ What in this last DVD session struck you as the most important,
the most relevant point?

When I first moved to Colorado years ago, I bought myself a fly-
fishing rod and reel and just went out on a river to teach myself. After
fruitless hours of watching fish swim by, a nearby fishing guide who
was enjoying a day off offered me the instruction I needed. He con-
cluded our impromptu time with a fatherly "That's the way it's done,
son." As I got into the car and drove away, I knew that God had fathered
me through this man.

❖ Who is God using to father you in the following areas of your life?

- In your walk with God?

- In your finances and budgeting?

- In your marriage?

- In parenting your children?

- In a hobby or sport?

- In your career?

- In health and lifestyle issues?

- In working with mechanical things (cars, chainsaws, plumbing, etc.)?

❖ If there is no one fathering you, in what area of life would you love to be fathered?

Looking back over my life, I can see times when I've simply been striving to show that I have what it takes. Other times I've focused on indulging my comforts—eating dinner out, buying the latest "toys," or taking exotic vacations. For much of my life I've felt that I'm on my own in making life work, and if any good is going to come my way, I have to make it happen myself.

❖ Which is your greater battle—"striving" or "indulgence"?

❖ How have striving and indulgence shown themselves in your life?

For years I wasn't sure how I felt about God as my Father. Instead of focusing on God's true qualities, I found that I was transferring all my feelings about my earthly father to my heavenly one.

❖ What immediately comes to mind when I ask you, "What qualities of your earthly father have you transferred to God?"

❖ Of these qualities, which do you need to correct in order to have a proper perspective of God? How will you do that?

What we're trying to do through this series is reorient the way we look at life and see that we are men in need of fathering and initiation. We need to know that God is our Father coming to us to take us on this journey.

❖ Where are you on the continuum of seeing God as a Father who's coming to take you on your masculine journey? Explain.

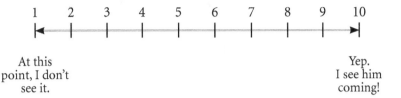

1   2   3   4   5   6   7   8   9   10

At this
point, I don't
see it.

Yep.
I see him
coming!

One of the ways God honors us as men is that he often waits for us to be intentional, to be engaged in the process. Our journey of masculine initiation isn't a spectator sport! We must be intentional in putting ourselves into situations where we know we need initiation. We need to start saying yes to the invitation to play basketball, to the offers of getting help with finances or the car, or to the request of seeing a marriage counselor.

❖ Why must we be intentional in our masculine journey?

❖ What is the difference between striving and being intentional? Where do you draw the line between the two?

At any point in a man's life, as God is working deeply with him through the six stages on the journey of masculine restoration, something needs to be dismantled and something needs to be healed. What needs to be dismantled is the fatherless way we live, the recklessness or hiding that characterizes our lives. What needs to be healed is a genuine masculine strength. This is the very mission of Christ: to heal our broken hearts, to set us free from all bondage and to make us into "oaks of righteousness, a planting of the LORD for the display of his splendor" (Isaiah 61:3).

❖ Where do "oaks of righteousness" grow and blossom in your life?

❖ How will you now seek out the initiation you need?

CLOSING THOUGHTS AND PRAYER

Press play on your DVD player. The remaining portion of the video will lead you through a few final thoughts and a prayer.

Let us consider how we may spur one another on toward love and good deeds. Let us not give up meeting together, as some are in the habit of doing, but let us encourage one another.

—Hebrews 10:24–25

GOING DEEPER

❖ As this DVD series ends, what have you learned, thought about, or pondered when it comes to the generosity of God's heart for you?

❖ Think about each of the six stages of our masculine journey and answer the following questions about them. Was this stage cut short in your journey, or were you wounded in this stage? What are you hoping for God to do in you regarding this stage? What are you hearing or yearning to hear from God about this stage?

• Boyhood Stage

• Cowboy Stage

• Warrior Stage

• Lover Stage

• King Stage

• Sage Stage

What I've come to see is that the joy and life God wants to bring us are the things most fiercely opposed by Satan. But of course, now that I think about it—isn't that just what Jesus said? He links them in the same verse: "The thief comes only to steal and kill and destroy; I have come that they may have life, and have it to the full" (John 10:10).

❖ As you have gone through this DVD series, have you identified the assaults the enemy has set against you and your joy? What are they? How will you counter them?

Jesus enjoyed a relationship with his Father that we crave. Not a stained-glass churchy sort of formality, but masculine oneness. They were close, so close that they were One. We were made for the very same thing, and our lives just aren't right until we have it. Jesus wants us to enjoy oneness *with the Father*, and we need oneness with the Father. *This* is the healing of the masculine soul.

❖ How has your desire for and understanding of "intimacy with God" developed or changed as you've gone through this series? Consider John 17:21–23 in your answer.

❖ What is needed to thrust you forward in your journey?

All masculine initiation is ultimately spiritual. The tests and challenges, the joys and adventures are all designed to awaken a man's soul, draw him into contact with the masculine in himself, in other men, in the world, and in God as Father. But most men share the perception that God is found in church, and that the rest of life is . . . just the rest of life. The tragedy of this is that the rest of life seems far more attractive to them than church, and thus God seems removed and even opposed to the things that make them come alive. We must recover the wildness of our spirituality.

❖ In being intentional, what adventure do you hope to live in this next season?

❖ Do you have a desire to lead a group of men through this material or to continue with your current group of men on another topic?

Our life *is* a quest, my brothers, arranged by our Father for our initiation. There are gifts along the way to remind us that we are his beloved sons. Adventures to call forth the cowboy, and battles to train the warrior. There is Beauty to awaken the lover, and power on behalf of others to prepare the king. A lifetime of experience from which the sage will speak. The masculine journey, traveled for millennia by men before us. And now, my brothers, the trail calls us on. Remember this:

I will not leave you as orphans; I will come to you.
. . . My Father will love [you], and we will come
to [you] and make our home with [you].
—John 14:18, 23

PRAYER

As you pray, ask God to cement the lessons he's taught you during the last eight weeks and over the course of your lifetime, that you may continue to grow in your masculine journey.

———&⟨⟩&———

O God, dear Jesus . . . thank you for all you have done in my life thus far. Lord, I hunger and thirst for more! More courage, more conviction, more healing, more vision, more of you. Guide me on this masculine journey. Father me. Initiate me. Validate me. Make me the man you designed me to be. When I falter, quicken me. When I fail, encourage me again. And as I move into my true strength and my true place in your great story, O God, all the praise and glory will be to you. I am in this for good. In Jesus' name. Amen.

NOTES

A NOTE
FROM THE AUTHOR

Having just finished this eight-week series as a group of men, the obvious question is, where do you go from here? I think my first offer of counsel to you would be to read *Fathered by God* again! There is no way you have gotten all that God has for you in one reading. The scope of the journey is too great, and our needs for validation, direction, healing, and initiation too great to perceive all at once.

Another great resource is *Wild at Heart*. Every man was once a boy. And every little boy has dreams, big dreams. But what happens to those dreams when they grow up? *Wild at Heart* invites men to recover their masculine heart, defined in the image of a passionate God. Get a few guys together and go through the book as a Band of Brothers. There is a Participant's Guide and a Study Manual available for that book as well. These materials come alongside those men who long to have a guide to lead them through the recovery of their masculine heart. Filled with personal stories, illustrations from popular movies and books, and probing questions, this material will set you on a heart-searching expedition to become the man God sees and made you to be.

Then what? Come to Ransomedheart.com and you will find many tools and maps for your initiation, like our audio series *The Hope of Prayer* and *The Utter Relief of Holiness*. We offer camps and retreats for men, and podcasts. Come and continue the journey!

Of course, you know now that my counsel will always first and foremost be, "Ask God." He knows what you need next. Ask him what he has for you—what friends, what adventures, what battles, what help he has in store. Be intentional. "Those who are led by the Spirit of God are sons of God" (Romans 8:14).

APPENDIX: A DAILY PRAYER FOR FREEDOM

My dear Lord Jesus, I come to you now to be restored in you—to renew my place in you, my allegiance to you, and to receive from you all the grace and mercy I so desperately need this day. I honor you as my sovereign Lord, and I surrender every aspect of my life totally and completely to you. I give you my body as a living sacrifice; I give you my heart, soul, mind, and strength; and I give you my spirit as well. I cover myself with your blood—my spirit, my soul, and my body. And I ask your Holy Spirit to restore my union with you, seal me in you, and guide me in this time of prayer. In all that I now pray, I include [my wife and/or my children, by name]. Acting as [her or their] head, I bring them under my authority and covering, and I come under your authority and covering. Holy Spirit, apply to [her or them] all that I now pray on their behalf.

Dear God, holy and victorious Trinity, you alone are worthy of all my worship, my heart's devotion, all my praise and all my trust and all the glory of my life. I worship you, bow to you, and give myself over to you in my heart's search for life. You alone are Life, and you have become my life. I renounce all other gods, all idols, and I give you the place in my heart and in my life that you truly deserve. I confess here and now that it is all about you, God, and not about me. You are the Hero of this story, and I belong to you. Forgive me, God, for my every sin. Search me and know me, and reveal to me any aspect of my life that is not pleasing to you. Expose any agreements I have made, and grant me the grace of a deep and true repentance.

Heavenly Father, thank you for loving me and choosing me before you made the world. You are my true Father—my Creator, my Redeemer, my Sustainer, and the true end of all things, including my life. I love you; I trust you; I worship you. Thank you for proving your love for me by sending your only Son, Jesus, to be my substitute and representative. I receive him and all his life and all his work, which you ordained for me. Thank you for including me in Christ, for forgiving me my sins, for granting me his righteousness, for making me complete in him. Thank you for making me alive with Christ, raising me with him, seating me with him at your right hand, granting me his authority, and anointing me with your Holy Spirit. I receive it all with thanks and give it total claim to my life.

Jesus, thank you for coming for me, for ransoming me with your own life. I honor you as my Lord; I love you, worship you, and trust you. I sincerely receive you as my redemption, and I receive all the work and triumph of your crucifixion, whereby I am cleansed from all my sin through your shed blood, my old nature is removed, my heart is circumcised unto God, and every claim being made against me is disarmed. I take my place in your cross and death, whereby I have died with you to sin and to my flesh, to the world, and to the evil one. I am crucified with Christ, and I have crucified my flesh with all its passions and desires. I take up my cross and crucify my flesh with all its pride, unbelief, and idolatry. I put off the old man. I now bring the cross of Christ between me and all people, all spirits, all things.

Holy Spirit, apply to me [my wife and/or children] the fullness of the work of the crucifixion of Jesus Christ for me. I receive it with thanks and give it total claim to my life.

Jesus, I also sincerely receive you as my new life, my holiness and sanctification, and I receive all the work and triumph of your resurrection, whereby I have been raised with you to a new life, to walk in newness of life, dead to sin and alive to God. I am crucified with Christ, and it is no longer I who live but Christ who lives in me. I now take my place in your resurrection, whereby I have been made alive with you. I reign in life through you. I now put on the new man in all holiness and humility, in all righteousness and purity and truth. Christ is now my life, the one who strengthens me. Holy Spirit, apply to me [my wife and/or my children] the fullness of the resurrection of Jesus Christ for me. I receive it with thanks and give it total claim to my life.

Jesus, I also sincerely receive you as my authority and rule, my everlasting victory over Satan and his kingdom, and I receive all the work and triumph of your ascension, whereby Satan has been judged and cast down, his rulers and authorities disarmed. All authority in heaven and on earth given to you, Jesus, and I have been given fullness in you, the Head over all. I take my place in your ascension, whereby I have been raised with you to the right hand of the Father and established with you in all authority.

I bring your authority and your kingdom rule over my life, my family, my household, and my domain.

And now I bring the fullness of your work—your cross, resurrection, and ascension—against Satan, against his kingdom, and against all his emissaries and all their work warring against me and my domain. Greater is he who is in me than he who is in the world. Christ has given me authority to overcome all the power of the evil one, and I claim that authority now over and against every enemy, and I banish them in the name of Jesus Christ. Holy Spirit, apply to me [my wife and/or my children] the fullness of the work of the ascension of Jesus Christ for me. I receive it with thanks and give it total claim to my life.

Holy Spirit, I sincerely receive you as my Counselor, my Comforter, my Strength, and my Guide. Thank you for sealing me in Christ. I honor you as my Lord, and I ask you to lead me into all truth, to anoint me for all of my life and walk and calling, and to lead me deeper into Jesus today. I fully open my life to you in every dimension and aspect—my body, my soul, and my spirit—choosing to be filled with you, to walk in step with you in all things. Apply to me, blessed Holy Spirit, all of the work and all of the gifts in pentecost. Fill me afresh, blessed Holy Spirit. I receive you with thanks and give you total claim to my life [and my wife and/or children].

Heavenly Father, thank you for granting to me every spiritual blessing in the heavenlies in Christ Jesus. I receive those blessings into my life today, and I ask the Holy Spirit to bring all those blessings into my life this day. Thank you for the blood of Jesus. Wash me once more with his blood from every sin and stain and evil device. I put on your armor—the belt of truth, the breastplate of righteousness, the shoes of the readiness of the gospel of peace, the helmet of salvation. I take up the shield of faith and the sword of the Spirit, the Word of God, and I wield these weapons against the evil one in the power of God. I choose to pray at all times in the Spirit, to be strong in you, Lord, and in your might.

Father, thank you for your angels. I summon them in the authority of Jesus Christ and release them to war for me and my household. May they guard me at all times this day.

Thank you for those who pray for me; I confess I need their prayers, and I ask you to send forth your Spirit and rouse them, unite them, raising up the full canopy of prayer and intercession for me. I call forth the kingdom of the Lord Jesus Christ this day throughout my home, my family, my life, and my domain. I pray all of this in the name of Jesus Christ, with all glory and honor and thanks to him.

NOTES

Introduction

1. John Eldredge, *Fathered by God* (Nashville: Thomas Nelson, 2009), 1–3.

Session 1

1. Eldredge, *Fathered by God*, 7.
2. Ibid., 6–7.

Session 3

1. Eldredge, *Fathered by God*, 79–80.

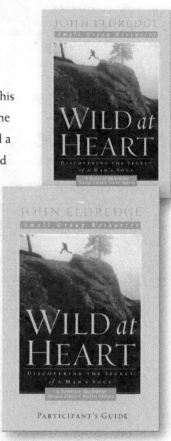

CAPTIVATING: HEART to HEART

Small Group Video Series

JOHN ELDREDGE & STASI ELDREDGE

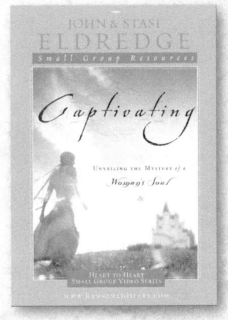

Every woman in her heart of hearts longs to be romanced, to play an irreplaceable role in a great adventure, and to unveil beauty. God placed these desires in women's hearts to help them discover who they are meant to be, the role that is theirs to play, and to draw them more deeply into his heart.

Join Stasi Eldredge and her friends in ten sessions of honest and vulnerable conversation, teaching, and discovery. Through their laughter and tears, their prayers and wisdom, you'll find God drawing you into the life he meant for you to live as a woman!

Perfect for individuals, churches, and small groups, the *Captivating: Heart to Heart Small Group Video Series* will guide you through the adventure of rediscovering the romance, the adventure, and the beauty God set within every woman's heart.

Contents include:

- Ten sessions on five DVDs
- CD-ROM containing Facilitator's Guide and promotional materials
- *Captivating: Heart to Heart Study Guide* sold separately

DVD Kit ISBN: 978-1-4185-4183-5
Study Guide ISBN: 978-1-4185-2754-9

Printed in the USA
CPSIA information can be obtained
at www.ICGtesting.com
JSHW011736200624
65123JS00001B/32